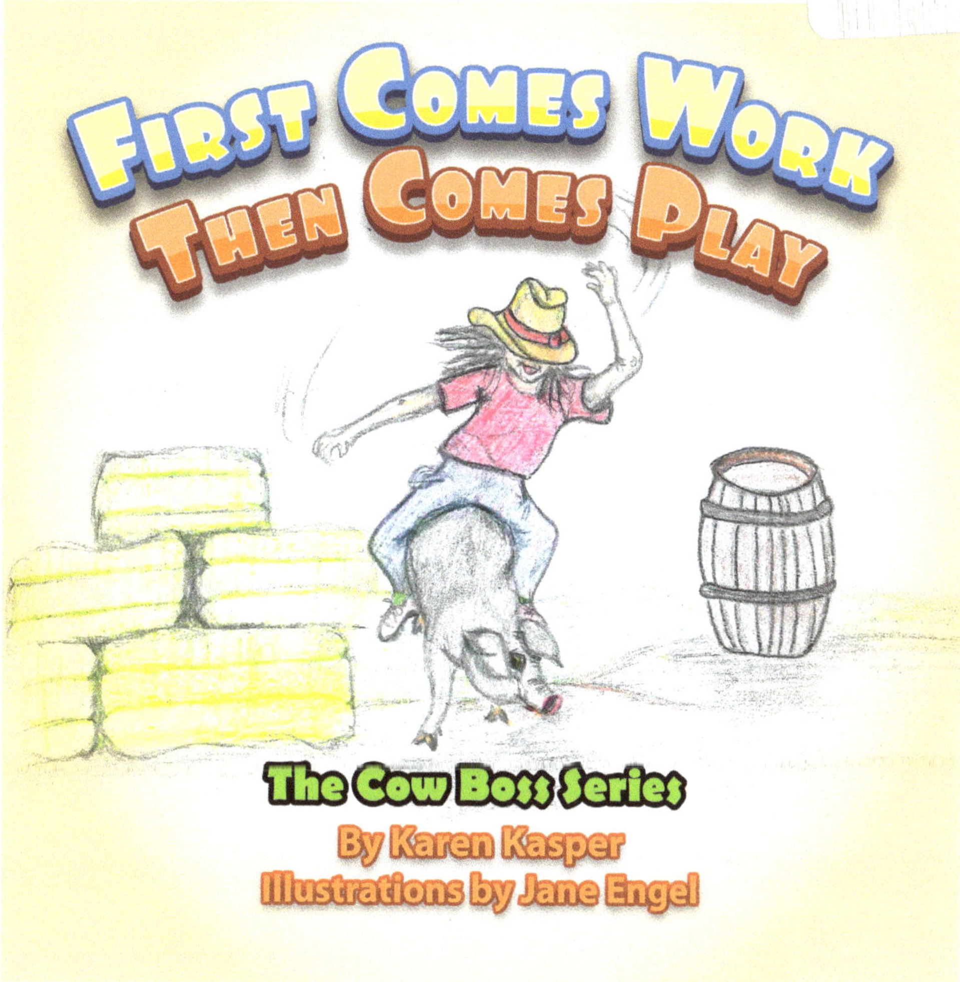

First Comes Work Then Comes Play

The Cow Boss Series

By Karen Kasper
Illustrations by Jane Engel

Copyright © 2017 Karen Kasper
Illustrated by Jane Engel
All rights reserved.

No part of this book may be reproduced in any manner without the written consent of the publisher except for brief excerpts in critical reviews or articles.

ISBN 13: 978-1-61244-570-0
Library of Congress Control Number: 2017911440

Printed in the United States of America

Halo Publishing International
1100 NW Loop 410
Suite 700 - 176
San Antonio, Texas 78213
Toll Free 1-877-705-9647
www.halopublishing.com
e-mail: contact@halopublishing.com

I'm honored and excited for you to meet the rest of my family. Farmer Pete is my husband. This book features our son, Tony, and daughters, Caitlin and Stephanie, along with grandson, Milo.

Over the years, the kids taught me to appreciate the small things and a lot about creativity. They developed a great sense of imagination, independence, work ethic, entrepreneurship and a great respect for agriculture.

Also, thanks to my dear friend, Jane, for bringing our old family photos back to life. These pictures depict some of the work tasks and creative things our kids did while growing up.

The spring rains make potholes in the driveway. Dad says, "It's time to help me smooth them out with the road grader." Tony feels lucky. This job is actually fun.

The 4-wheeler stays parked until the driveway is smoothed out. That's the rule!

The chickens happily coo and cluck because they hear Stephanie coming. They know this means fresh food and water. Mom says, "Carefully put the eggs into the basket so they don't break."

Milo enjoys coloring and decorating those white and brown eggs.
Do you think it would be a good idea to boil the eggs before coloring them?

Wilbur likes a cool shower on hot summer days. Somebody filled up the swimming pool before giving Wilbur his shower. Oops, he isn't going to wait any longer! That's a good lesson, that work comes before play!

Since the pool is occupied; the kids wonder what they could do to cool off. They decide the next best thing is a water tank. It's cozy but better than nothing. What do you think they will do differently next time?

The cows were very hungry today and ate all their hay. Dad says, "Feed them more." The cows are happy and give a little nudge to say thank you.

Since all the work is done, it's okay to enjoy a short nap.
Even Charlie is tired out.

Charlie helps clean up the branches that last night's storm blew down. He has also learned that everyone must pitch in when there is work to do.

A well-deserved gator ride is in order after working so hard. The dogs think this is great.

It is summer, and dad always says, "We have to make hay when the sun shines." This job takes many long days and nights. The cows sure do love that hay!

Let the pig riding begin! The hay is baled and stacked, so mom says, "Go and have some fun."
Do you think she meant pig riding?

Many pine cones must be picked up before mowing. Mom offered to pay five cents for every cone. There were 1,771 to be exact! Why do you think the kids counted them?

Once the pinecones were collected, the lawn was beautifully mown. What a nice arena for riding Nellie, or not?

The state fair is coming soon. All summer long, Lucille got her daily walk and bath. She is calm, clean and silky for the show. Mom reminds us that there is a lot of work to do if we want to take cows to the fair.

Steph is so proud of her Supreme Champion trophy!
Do you think it was worth all that work?

In the fall, leaves must be raked up. Mom says, "If everybody pitches in, it will go faster. Then you can have free time."

Jumping in the leaves is fun. Hiding in them is even more fun. Leaping off the swing into the leaf pile is the most fun! Shhh...don't tell mom.

The best part of fall is picking pumpkins. It's a contest to find the most goofy-shaped gourds and the biggest pumpkin. We are proud of our harvest. We will sell some, give some away and...

We will also carve and paint some. A few pumpkins get funny faces and some get spooky faces. Charlie wants to help too.

Wow, winter brought 12 inches of snow. Everyone grabs a shovel. "Hey who threw that snowball?" asks Steph. Tony replies, "Dad always says find a way to make the work fun."

Now it's free time...let's have a sleigh ride! We have no Santa, sleigh or reindeer, but Tony takes care of that. He makes a harness out of twine string, puts it on a Jersey cow and finds the sled. He hollers "We're ready, hop on Caitlin and Stephanie!"

www.ingramcontent.com/pod-product-compliance
Lightning Source LLC
Chambersburg PA
CBHW041439040426
42453CB00021B/2463